Jurassic Way

A walk through Northamptonshire

Julia Thorley

For everyone I pass along the way,
especially those who keep their dog on a lead.

Contents

Wardington – Chacombe – Middleton Cheney – Overthorpe – Warkworth – Banbury

1. Best foot forward
Finding your way among the fossils

If you play golf, you will know that you can park your trolley outside the clubhouse secure in the knowledge that it will still be there when you come out again. If you ski, it is extremely unlikely that anyone will tamper with your equipment if you leave it outside a café while you top up your glühwein levels. Likewise, if you're trekking across the outback or driving through some inner-continental wilderness, when you meet someone coming the other way you will stop and each check that the other is ok for, say, water. It's common courtesy.

There are similar unwritten rules for walking in the English countryside, which is why on a walk along the Jurassic Way in Northamptonshire when I saw an organised group heading towards me I got ready to acknowledge a kindred spirit with a nod and a smile. How did I know they were an organised party? Because the chap at the front with a map around his neck secured in a waterproof clipboard was clearly striding out with more confidence than the posse behind him. He was wearing unnecessary gaiters and, the biggest clue of all, he had a flag poking out of the back of his rucksack and extending several feet above his head. This seemed a little over the top, literally and metaphorically, given the lack of gradient, tortuous terrain or wild animals.

Clearly, the intrepid explorers were not going to slow down as they reached me for fear of losing sight of their leader. Nevertheless, I stepped to one side and opened my mouth to say a cheery hello. Unfortunately, I forgot to remove my invisibility cloak and they steamed past, heads down, without registering my presence at all. Well, that was just rude.

At this juncture, I must reassure you that most of the natives of Northamptonshire are friendly, or at the very least non-threatening. That is one of the reasons why walking the Jurassic Way is such a lovely way to spend your time. The obvious thing to point out is that this is not the South West Coast Path that encompasses the Jurassic Coast. The only thing the two footpaths have in common is geology.

It is the rock beneath that gives the footway its name, being from the Jurassic Period and therefore 140–195 million years old, a time when Northamptonshire was covered by shallow tropical seas. The waymarkers along the route feature a 'seashell' logo, which is actually a brachiopod called Kallirhynchia sharpi, named after Samuel Sharp, a Victorian scientist and fossil collector who lived in Northampton. He discovered that this particular fossil was abundant in the rock beds in the middle of the Jurassic system and was therefore an extremely useful tool when dating rocks.

Much of the footpath is over gentle rolling hills that are quintessentially English, but every now and then it breaks out into stony ground that offers an excellent opportunity for fossil-hunting. If you intend to walk this route with a geologist in tow, be prepared for lots of stops to examine the ground through a hand lens, because once you get your eye in you will see traces of ferns, bones and shells from creatures such as coral, bivalves and brachiopods. Many is the time I've given up waiting and walked on, leaving Mr Thorley on his hands and knees peering at some long-dead sea creature.

As a general rule, it is fine to pick up examples that are just loose on the path, but you mustn't set to with hammer and chisel. There is excellent advice to be had from United Kingdom Amateur Fossil Hunters. If you want to find out more about the rocks beneath your feet, the British Geological Survey has maps and resources, some of which are free to view online. Also, check out the iGeology app, which is a colourful guide to bedrock geology, superficial deposits and more besides.

If you're really into fossils, you might like to know that the church of St Helen in Great Oxendon (on our route) is the resting place of John Morton, former rector of that parish, who in 1712 published his *Natural History of Northamptonshire*. He devoted more than 60 pages to fossils and went into great detail about the differences between scallops and ammonites.

Our Jurassic Way is 88 miles long and it begins in Stamford (which is technically just over the border north into Lincolnshire) and finishes in Banbury (just over the border south into Oxfordshire). I know what you're thinking: 'Northamptonshire? There's nothing there except the M1, the A14 and a lot of warehouses.' It's true that the county is at the heart of the so-called logistics golden triangle, but if you think it's a place that's only worth passing through on the way to somewhere more interesting, then you're wrong. This is the county of spires and squires.

If you like your architecture there is plenty to please you. In many places it is picture-postcard pretty, with houses made from local stone and topped with thatch, and even the tiniest villages have substantial churches. As for the squires, there are several grand homes along or near the route, the most celebrated of which is probably Rockingham Castle. Visitors with an interest in the Civil War should note that Rockingham was held by a garrison of Roundhead soldiers. There are other links with wars and battles to explore along the route.

If history is not your thing, there are plenty of opportunities for spotting wildlife. One of the most successful breeding programmes of recent years has been the saving of the red kite. By 1871, this magnificent bird was extinct in England, but after a successful campaign to reintroduce it, it often feels as though it is a more common sight in the Northamptonshire skies than the sparrow.

This book isn't a 'turn left, turn right' sort of guidebook, but rather a gentle overview of what the Jurassic Way has to offer along its 88 miles, with a few editorial asides. The footpath lends itself to being walked in bite-sized chunks, because it passes through lots of villages and some larger towns that provide convenient stopping-off points. The entire route is extremely well signposted, but, this notwithstanding, it is a good idea to take the relevant Ordnance Survey maps with you.

Best maps for the job are the OS Explorer series, 1:25,000 scale (which is 4cm to 1km/2.5in to 1 mile). The good news is that many OS maps now come with a digital version that can be downloaded to a smartphone or tablet, which saves you having to manipulate huge sheets of paper in the wind.

The maps that cover this route are:

- 234 for the Stamford to Harringworth leg
- 224 Gretton to Stoke Albany
- 223 Stoke Wood to Watford
- 222 Ashby St Ledgers to Staverton
- 206 Lower Catesby to Warkworth
- 191 for the last leg to Banbury Lock (although since the footpath is very clearly marked and follows the towpath, you could get away without this one) – and actually there is a tiny bit missing between 206 and 191, where the path follows the boundary of a field between pages.

Occasionally boundaries will have disappeared, so the map doesn't exactly match what you can see. One day, Mr Thorley and I ended up crossing a massive field in completely the wrong direction, partly because it had been recently ploughed and the footpath had disappeared, but partly because we didn't refer closely enough to the map. After much huffing and puffing we returned to the last point we were sure of – that is, right back at the start of the field – and got our bearings again. Courage in hands, we set off in a straight line across the bumpy terrain that went from ploughed furrows to cereal stubble. Sure enough, we picked up the signs for the Jurassic Way again.

Looking back the route was clear, but from our starting point it was a bit of a leap of faith. That was half a mile we needn't have walked.

In my frivolous moments, walking the Jurassic Way makes me think perhaps I should stomp along like a stegosaurus. In much the same way, on a recent trip to Devon we were encouraged to walk the Coleridge Way, which presumably means writing a Romantic epic poem as we go along.

Much of Northamptonshire's countryside is inaccessible to the public as it is either in the ownership of private estates or used as arable farmland. If you want to explore this hidden treasure, the Jurassic Way is the best way. Note, please, that places change without warning. Pubs go out of business, houses become flats, firms relocate and shops close down. I've done my best to be accurate and up to date, but readers are advised they are responsible for their own wellbeing.

2. Clothing dilemmas, Pocket Parks and Collyweston slate
Stamford – Easton-on-the-Hill – Ketton – Duddington

The Jurassic Way begins in the beautiful town of Stamford. On our maiden trip, the first job when we got there was to seek out an outdoor clothing shop to buy a belt for Mr Thorley's walking trousers, which were threatening to fall down. This proved more difficult than expected, but in the end he settled for what we were told was a rucksack compression webbing strap with quick side-release buckle. Whatever it was, it did the job.

Tricky thing clothing. I was the eldest of three children. There is no doubt that my dad loved us all equally, albeit in a 'show, don't tell' sort of way but nor can there be any doubt that he didn't really understand me. My two brothers were encouraged – if not obliged – to follow him around first with hammers and screwdrivers from a My First Tool Box, then later with the real thing and ultimately with a dangerous selection of power tools. However, on the rare occasions Mum left him in sole charge of the three of us he didn't have a role for me. Very much a product of his upbringing, he believed that girls didn't do DIY. As it turns out, he was right in my case. Perhaps my desire to be one of the lads is the reason why I gravitated towards scruffy clothes that it didn't matter if I got dirty.

Re-reading this, I see that I seem to have settled on to the therapist's couch, but the deviation came to mind because I was thinking how comfy walking clothes are and how I am happy to dress for practical reasons, rather than style, when there is a footpath to be conquered. I don't mean I go out looking like a bag of spanners, but I'm never going to be the sort of woman who can do 15 miles in a Staffordshire gale and look as though I've just stepped out of a beauty salon. No, give me some reliable boots and the right number of layers and I'm good to go.

It starts with underwear, which must be well fitting and supportive in all the right places. I once did a walk with a group in which one chap had to keep stopping to, shall we say, adjust, because he had 'put the wrong pants on'. A little grappling and the shake of a leg and he was ok to set off again, but it was a recurring theme for the whole day.

I favour leggings if it's muddy, tucked into my socks, but proper walking trousers suit me down to the ground – literally. I have come to the conclusion that I am a size 11. Size 10 is OK on a 'thin' day for posing for photos, but a bit risky if there's any high-stepping on the itinerary. Size 12 needs a belt, but is less likely to frighten the person following me over the stile. The trouble is they are often too long and my approach to sewing is that if I can't fix it with a stapler and/or Copydex, it doesn't get done. Hence I often fall foul of capillary action on wet days.

I have faulty wiring. My feet are always cold, so chunky socks are a must. I also have children's feet (size 3), so the only socks that fit me often come with

L and R on them, which is thoughtful. My stupidly small feet mean I generally have to buy children's boots, which is good because they're cheap, but bad because they're not meant to bear the weight of a stompy old lady like me. I struggle to buy proper shoes, too, especially to go with a smart outfit or a natty number for a night out, unless I want something that wouldn't be out of place at a Year 6 school disco.

On top I build layers to suit the season. Sometimes when we set off, Mr Thorley and I look as though we are planning to walk in separate climate zones; but as I always say, you can take it off, but you can't put it on if you haven't got it with you. For extreme cold I have an electronic pebble-shaped hand-warmer I can secrete in my pocket.

Back to the walk. The trouble with beginning in Stamford is that there is so much to see that it's tempting to spend the day there instead. You might struggle to tear yourself away from the stunning Georgian architecture, the listed buildings made of mellow local limestone, the medieval churches, the shops and eateries, the museum and the arts centre…

Stamford was the site of one of the Eleanor Crosses. In November 1290, Eleanor of Castile, Queen of England and wife of Edward I, died at Harby in Nottinghamshire. The king was devastated and decided that she would be buried in Westminster Abbey. Her body was taken to Lincoln for embalming and then a solemn procession escorted her on the journey south to her final resting place, accompanied by the king. The route was planned so that there would be a resting place approximately every 20 miles and the king decreed that at each of these places a cross should be erected in memory of his queen. These points were Grantham, Stamford, Geddington, Northampton, Stony Stratford, Woburn, Dunstable, St Albans, Waltham Abbey, West Cheam and Charing Cross. There is nothing remaining of the one at Stamford, but the one at Geddington in Northamptonshire (albeit a detour off the Jurassic Way) is well worth a visit.

But let us begin. Make your way to The Meadows down by the river Welland for the start of the walk. Off Bath Row, there is a stone monument denoting Venice Walk just beyond Lammas Bridge and before the George Bridge. Set off in the direction shown by the Public Bridleway marker, and you will find yourself sharing the path with the Macmillan Way and, later, the Hereward Way. This happens a lot, because the county is crisscrossed with many different marked routes, footpaths and bridleways. However, the Jurassic Way is well marked with its distinctive shell symbol.

You will reach a monument to Boudicca on the site of a Roman ford. There is an old Roman crossing point on the left, on a direct alignment with Ermine Street and now marked by a stone plaque.

Up ahead is the thunder of the mighty A1, at 410 miles the longest numbered road in the UK. It connects London with Edinburgh and for much of its route follows various branches of the historic Great North Road. Several sections of the route have been upgraded to motorway standard , but not that which flows past Stamford. Having driven on it many a time,

I can testify that it has some of the shortest and hence most terrifying slip roads I have ever encountered.

Fortunately there is a wide tunnel that takes walkers under the road, so you don't have to risk life and limb trying to cross it. It's worth standing for a moment to listen to the roar of the traffic overhead and give thanks to the engineers. You will, though, need your wits about you to cross the railway line, which goes from Birmingham to Peterborough. Then it's up the hill and away into the countryside towards Easton-on-the-Hill

You will enter Easton-on-the-Hill at the back of the Chartered Institute of Purchasing and Supply, which has thoughtfully created a Ramblers' Rest green space with picnic benches and a notice inviting us to 'Take a pew and enjoy the view.' The gesture was marred slightly by the fact that I managed to find an enormous dog turd, but I don't think CIPS can be blamed for that.

Once on the lane there is a local footpath that goes straight on across the fields, but you need to turn left and make your way into the village past All Saints Church, with its grand perpendicular tower with clasping buttresses and crocketed pinnacles. (You'll see a lot of these throughout the county.)

Stop when you get to the war memorial just past the Blue Bell pub and take a moment to read the inscription. As well as the usual tribute to those who lost their lives in the First and Second World Wars, there is also a particular acknowledgement of 'The Officers, NCO's [sic] and men of the Royal Air Force who were killed in or near this place during the year 1918'. The roll of honour is available online.

The Second World War also made its physical mark on the village. The Firs, a house on High Street (which used to be called Bell Street and is presumably where the pub got its name), lost its roof when a bomb fell straight through it. The front of the building still has a flat roof. The house is opposite the village hall, which was formerly the boys' school and retains its impressive tower that houses a Benson clock and bell tower. Years ago, I covered a yoga class here for a teacher-friend and although she had warned me, it still made me jump when the clock mechanism wound itself up to a frenzy at eight o'clock.

By the way, if you turn left at the pub instead, you can make your way to the Pocket Park (see below). Just when you think you're about to step on to the A43, the park is on your right. When you're ready to move on, either retrace your steps or take the path up the slope towards the back of the park. This brings you on to the main road for a short, but noisy walk as far as New Road on the right, which will take you past the village hall. At the end, turn left and walk back towards the pub to pick up the Jurassic Way again.

Northamptonshire's Pocket Parks

One delightful feature of the whole county is a series of Pocket Parks, an idea that originated in Northamptonshire. From the early 1980s to 2015, what was then Northamptonshire County Council worked in partnership with other organisations and local authorities to help local volunteer groups create over 70 Pocket Parks across the county. They vary in size from 0.04 hectares to 35 hectares and are found in all types of locations from town centres to quiet villages.

Pocket Parks are open areas of land that are owned and managed by local people, providing free, open access for all at all times and at the same time helping to protect and conserve local wildlife, heritage and landscape. Some of these are in odd corners of the county's towns, but there are several on or near the Jurassic Way, including in Gretton, West Haddon, Woodford Halse and Jetty Field in Braunston.

First on the Jurassic Way is in Easton-on-the-Hill, just off the High Street in a spot known locally as Spring Close. It isn't very big, but it does have a couple of benches. Until recently it also had a memorial in the form of a stone pyramid topped by a stone sphere, all built on a square base, and a triangular brass plate that bore a dedication to and the badge of the Polish Airborne Forces, a swooping eagle holding a victor's wreath. However, in November 2021 it was demolished by high winds and at the time of writing all there was to be seen was a pile of rubble.

In contrast, the one in Woodford Halse is a 17-acre reserve consisting of three disused railway cuttings that were once part of the Great Central Railway. The reserve is actively managed to prevent scrub invasion into areas of diverse grassland. The cuttings, which took four years to excavate prior to the opening of the railway in 1898, have been disused since 1966. Soils vary from ballast on the track bed to the calcareous strata higher in the embankments that support lime-loving plants. Rare wildflowers that grow there, include the orchids. County rarities including Adder's Tongue Fern and meadow saxifrage grow here, too. It is a haven for birds and wildlife.

A list of the Pocket Parks throughout the county is available online. This covers all the parks, even though Northamptonshire County Council no longer exists since 2021, when two unitary authorities – West Northants and North Northants – were created to replace the county council, which disappeared in a cloud of financial shame and scandal.

At the time of writing, we were able to pop into the Blue Bell Pub for a refreshing half, and I hope that it stays open for the foreseeable future. Locals there were forthcoming with information about the village, including the possibility of an alternative walk back to Stamford via the village of Wothorpe. This route goes close to the site of the disused ironstone quarry, which closed in the 1920s.

If you have time for a detour on your way out of Easton-on-the-Hill, go through the village to the nearby National Trust (NT) property. The Priest's House is one of the NT's smallest buildings. It was built by John Stokes, Rector of Easton from 1456 until he died in 1495. He left money for a chantry priest to pray for his soul. The priest could have lived here until 1545 when chantries became illegal following the dissolution of the monasteries and the funds were appropriated by the Crown. Later the house was used as a school, and the building underwent further alterations at the hand of Victorian architect Sir Thomas Jackson, who also designed the adjacent coach house. At the time of writing, the property is open daily, 10 to 5, but check before you set out, just in case. A noticeboard gives details of the keyholders who can give you access. It's well worth a visit not only for the building itself, but also because of the displays on local history it contains.

Walk through the village and then it's straight on down Ketton Drift track towards Ketton. I'm not going to lie: Mr Thorley and I find this part of the walk quite challenging not because of the terrain, which is flat, but because it seems to go on for ever.

On your right, spoiling the view somewhat but of huge local significance, is the Ketton Cement Works (or to give it its proper name, Hanson Cement Ketton, owned by HeidelbergCement). The works has been here since 1928 and its two kilns produce 14 million tonnes of cement every year, which is about 10% of the UK's total requirement. The area around Ketton is also noted for freestone, fine-grained stone that can be cut easily in any direction. Despite its rather grim appearance, Hanson Cement is keen to take care of the environment. The company says Ketton quarry is home to 26 different species of butterfly and a large number of birds, including nightingales. There is also a 207-foot-long bat cave in the quarry, and the company works closely with local conservation groups to protect the flora and fauna in its quarries.

Collyweston slate

South-east of Ketton is the village of Collyweston, which was once important for the mining and preparation of Collyweston slates. Mining took place there until the 1960s and the slates were a feature of homes and listed buildings across the country, including Northamptonshire, Lincolnshire, Cambridgeshire and Rutland. Strictly speaking, it isn't slate in the conventional sense; rather it is a form of limestone that can be worked like slate. Its distinctive colour and hard wearing characteristic made it a popular building material in the past but now it is scarce. In 2015 a bid was made to resume slate mining, and shortly afterwards it was announced that the mine would be reopening.

In 2016, a generation or so after it closed, Claude N Smith Ltd reopened a slate mine in the Northamptonshire village of Collyweston. Its website announced:

'CLAUDE N. SMITH, Specialist Collyweston Stone Slate Roofing with Slate Mine, Supplying and fixing Collyweston Slate from the only working Collyweston slate mine. (established 1965) To reach the new slate source miners had to remove over 100m of rock to form an access tunnel and are now producing Collyweston slate in abundance again.'

Our footpath doesn't go into the village of Ketton itself, but instead skirts round the hamlet of Geeston, within the parish of Ketton. We are now in Rutland, where we stay as the route roughly follows a path cut by the river Welland all the way into Duddington, where we are back in Northamptonshire.

Duddington is one of the loveliest villages in this part of the county. As you come across the fields towards it you will see a four-arch bridge, which dates from the 14th century. At its centre is an old metal sign marking the parish boundary between Duddington and Tixover. Cross over the bridge and on your right you will pass the site of the former mill, which last time we were there seemed to be undergoing some serious renovation. Continue up the hill along Mill Street as far as the High Street. There is no seashell sign to help you, but you need to turn right towards Bulwick and Weldon.

The houses in Duddington are simply stunning. Many have Collyweston slate on their roofs, though there are also quite a few thatched buildings. Here and elsewhere, by the way, note how so many such roofs are sagging, because Collyweston slate is very heavy compared to 'real' slate. Also of note in this village is the 12th-century church of St Mary, which contains traces of medieval wall paintings and one of the most impressive oak doors you'll see for miles around, decorated with remarkable metalwork.

The manor house (no longer there, sadly) was built in 1633 for one Nicholas Jackson and remained the home of that family for 300 years. Jackson was my maiden name and I wondered briefly if I could be related. What a turnup it would be if research proved that I owned Duddington! A girl can dream.

3. Café society, country wisdom and a rant about dogs
Duddington – Fineshade Wood – Wakerley – Barrowden – Harringworth – Gretton

When you've had your fill of lovely Duddington, head out of the village. When you see the Royal Oak on your left, turn right along the edge of the A43 until you see the cemetery on the other side of the road. Here you will have to take your life into your hands and cross over to the bridleway (there is a wooden fingerpost), then it's up the hill and away towards Fineshade Wood.

Fineshade, with Wakerley Great Wood, is one of the largest remnants of the former royal hunting ground Rockingham Forest. Once the playground of the nobility, today it is a working forest managed by Forestry England. The path skirts the edge of this lovely country park, which itself holds a series of easy-to-follow footpaths, cycle paths and bridleways, many of which are on gravel that are friendly to wheels and toddlers. However, there is also some tramping through fields and scrubland, but no stiles and it is all pretty accessible, with only a couple of gentle slopes – nothing that could be called a hill climb!

There is also a lovely visitor centre and café that is open all year round. We sat outside on an unseasonably mild November day, Mr Thorley with an enormous panini filled with barbecue chicken, bacon and cheese (why have one source of protein when you can have three) and I consumed my own bodyweight in tiffin. It was pleasing to see that the wooden tables had hooks under them for dog leads, or possibly toddler reins; perhaps this is always the case and I've just never noticed them.

Sighing with deep satisfaction I heard myself say, 'Ee, we've sat on some benches over the years.'

I have no idea where this ridiculous thought came from, but it made Mr Thorley laugh with gusto out of all proportion to the humour it contained.

On another walk – and not at this café, I must point out – we watched a woman and her Dachshund trot by and enter the café. (I have a problem with the term 'dog-friendly café', but don't get me started…). The pooch was sporting a very fetching little jacket and was quite cute. Moments later the waitress appeared with Mr Thorley's sausage bap in one hand and the dog's lead in the other.

'I'm just holding onto him while his owner's popped to the loo,' she explained.

I didn't say anything, but surely the dog could have been tied up outside? Is it me?

This seems as good a point as any to get something off my chest. To be clear, I have nothing against dogs. I can understand why people grow attached to their pets, and some dogs are really endearing and have outstanding personalities. Let us not forget, though, that dogs are animals; they act on instinct, not reason.

The other day, I stood rigid on the footpath while an unrestrained black mutt bounded up to me, leaping and barking.

When its owner caught up, he said, 'Believe it or not, he's frightened.'

'I know how it feels,' I retorted.

'Really!' said the man. 'There's no need for that attitude!'

I begged to differ.

Might I suggest that when out exercising your hound on a public footpath, should you see someone coming towards you, you call that hound to heel? Don't assume that everyone is happy to be jumped upon by a strange animal.

Nor does it help to say, 'Oh, he won't hurt you. He's just being friendly.'

How do you know he won't hurt me? Just because he's never bitten anyone yet, doesn't mean he won't start with me. Maybe he doesn't like the look of me. Maybe I smell intimidating. Maybe I'll accidentally make some movement that your animal will interpret as threatening. Second, I can be friendly, too, but I wouldn't leap up and gyrate against your leg or lick your face without being introduced first.

I'll say it again: dogs are animals. They are not people, no matter how much you wish they were. Broadly speaking, they have teeth at one end and smelly poo at the other. (I am of course ranting here against the minority. I'm sure everyone reading this is a responsible and considerate pet owner.)

Take your time exploring all that Fineshade has to offer; you could even hire a bike for a couple of hours. Depending on the time of year, you could be treated to swathes of snowdrops or bluebells. I wish I knew more about the natural world, because I'm sure I miss a lot as I take a walk through the countryside. I can identify the obvious things – hawthorn, oak tree, beech, ash – but what else is there, especially closer to the ground? Kedlock, nettles, dock leaves, brambles, stray growths of vibrant oil seed rape, sure; but what's that little blue flower? What sort of butterfly was that? What bird is singing out so beautifully – and where is it perched?

I have, though, recently learned that buttercups are toxic to cats, dogs, horses and goats. They won't do you much good if you eat them yourself, and can irritate the skin just by touching them. This has come as a huge surprise, as a think back to all the times I've held this pretty yellow flower under someone's chin to see if he or she liked butter!

I once accompanied a bat expert on a walk to identify and count species in a patch of woodland only a few miles from my home. I was given a set of headphones attached to a device that detected the slightest of bat noiscs and recorded the data for later analysis. I was given strict instructions not to speak and to keep my wits about me. I was also told to tuck my trouser bottoms into my boots 'just in case'. I didn't ask in case of what.

It was a fascinating experience. As well as the unearthly squeaks and calls of pipistrelles, there were other animal noises, too, and because we were walking carefully and in silence our path was crossed several times by deer. Unfortunately, the experience was cut short because the landowner was doing some logging in a nearby plantation, all bright lights and mega-machines. Even so, it was a very special experience with an aspect of nature I never expected to encounter.

All that said, it's time to follow the path out of the formal country park and towards the site of Fineshade Abbey and St Mary's Priory. Look right for faint remains of building works and the fishpond.

Cross the A43 again and go through Laxton Lodge gates. These were built in 1824 for the Laxton Estate and are Grade II listed. Continue up to the top of the hill and into Wakerley Great Wood (though actually it's Adams Wood on one side of the path and St Mary's Wood on the other). There are plenty of crisscross tracks to explore if you have the time, or simply trek on towards the car park and picnic tables. A point to note if you're driving here as your starting point is that the northerly of the two parking places indicated on the OS map is no longer there. This is now the entrance to the relatively new Wakerley Quarry currently being worked by Mick George. The area was previously the disused Spanhoe airfield dating from the Second World War. Before that, the area was arable land, but before that it was part of Rockingham Forest.

As you emerge at the other edge of the wood, the path runs alongside the medieval Church of Saint John the Baptist, now under the care of the Churches Conservation Trust, whose website says: 'Inside, it has a spectacular 12th-century chancel arch (look for the zig-zag pattern), which rests on some of the most beautiful carved capitals in England. The robust font is from the thirteenth century.'

Wakerley village is just below you at the foot of the hill, and it is pretty much a single street. The Jurassic Way follows the main road, but if you turn right on to

Waverly Road you will be on the Rutland Road, which nevertheless brings you eventually into Barrowden.

Otherwise, to leave Wakerley, follow the Jurassic Way as it takes a sharp right and go under the dismantled railway. There is no marked path along the railway, but we took a sneaky scramble up on to it, and there did seem to be an unofficial path. However, I recommend you continue the legitimate way across the field – very boggy at times – then take the footbridge over the Welland into Barrowden.

You will come out by the site of the old mill. There is a comprehensive information board from which I gleaned that first reports of a mill on the site date from 1259. It operated until 1925 and was eventually demolished in the 1970s. The tannery, which was behind the mill, is honoured in the house name on the site, which you will pass on your way along Main Street in a moment.

The path skirts the southern edge of the village as though heading to Morcott, but instead takes a sharp left. (Should you choose to go straight on instead, you will find you are following the Rutland Round.)

Many of the buildings of Barrowden are built from local limestone and extremely pretty. The charm of the village is added to by the presence of a quintessentially English duckpond. Take a slight detour here; turn left and walk down towards St Peter's Church. Just before the churchyard on the left is a modern-looking building called Apple Tree Cottage (not Church Cottage, as the village website has it), which has a stone plaque built into the wall in which is inscribed, 'why looks thou on my dust in passing by thou seest noe wonder thou thyselfe must die,' a sobering thought in reference, apparently, to the passing of funerals.

Mr Thorley and I took advantage of the lovely view from the churchyard to sit a moment and ponder our own mortality. It seems a church service hadn't long finished and a few dawdling parishioners passed us, many giving us a smile and a wave.

Across in the distance, beyond the impressive arches of the dismantled railway, we could see what looked like what might have been the humps and bumps of an abandoned settlement, but there was nothing on the map to confirm this. We accosted a couple of passing locals and asked if they could shed any light on the subject. They were able to tell us they were the remains of iron workings, pre-smelting works for sending to Corby: 'Definitely not built and operated by POWs during the First World War,' the gent told us, with a knowing look. 'That never happened.' Nuff said.

When you're ready, retrace your steps to the duckpond and then turn left. Along this road, we were intrigued to see that one house has a plaque on it commemorating 100 years of Thomas Cook Travel. If anyone knows why, I should be glad to know. According to the museum in nearby Market Harborough, he was living in that town when he launched the first pre-paid inclusive travel offer in 1840, a rail excursion from Leicester to a Temperance meeting in Loughborough.

Turn left to pick up the track again then head of to the right across the fields. Note, that the last time we were there, the signpost indicated the Rutland Round, but rest assured this is the way you need to walk. The route out takes you downhill then parallel (ish) with the river to the delightfully named Turtle Bridge, then on to Harringworth.

Our footpath skirts the eastern edge of the village. You will cross the road and pick up the path back across the fields. However, look to your left and there in the distance, across the top of the stables and towards the church, is the mighty Welland Valley Viaduct (known locally as the Harringworth Viaduct, not surprisingly). Even if you're not a railway enthusiast, I urge you to take a detour to get up close and personal with it. Instead of following the Jurassic Way, turn left and walk down Gretton Road. You will pass the remains of the old market cross, believed to date from the 14th century. Keep going past the turn for the village hall and in about three-quarters of a mile you will be able to go through a gate on to the field in which the viaduct stands.

The viaduct stretches across nearly the whole Welland Valley. Work began in March 1876 and the whole structure was finished just two years later, by the end of 1878. Total cost was £12,000, which is about £14 million in today's money. It was built to carry the London & Midland Railway and comprises 82 arches, each 40 feet wide. The foundations are concrete and the structure is faced with blue Staffordshire bricks (which pleases me, as a native of that county). Other bricks were manufactured on the ground at nearby Penn Green, Corby. It is still used by passenger and freight trains and is a popular spot for enthusiasts to stand with their cameras waiting for a glimpse of special excursion trains, often steam-hauled. The village station is, of course, long closed. It is a private property now, perched up on the hill a little further down and almost hidden from view.

Until we walked the Jurassic Way, Mr Thorley had never seen the viaduct before: shameful, really, when you consider it is only a few miles from where we live. He was bowled over by it and his joy was further enhanced by the sight of a long freight train passing by as we stood there.

Drag yourself away from this marvel of British engineering and retrace your steps, past the many beautiful properties in Harringworth. Re-join the footpath and make your way back towards Shotley, a tiny hamlet that is part of the Harringworth community. If you don't fancy the detour suggested above, there is a cracking view of the viaduct from here. Then head off up the hill for a straightforward walk across open countryside. You are now walking across what was once a deer park, created by William de Cantelupe (yes, really) in the 13th century. Jink around Harringworth Lodge and then keep the woods on your left. Studying the OS map, I was tickled to see that a stretch of trees just off the route is called Mavis Wood, which sounds like someone my mother might have gone to school with. A right and a left, and you come into Gretton.

Jurassic Way

4. Land-owners, changing times and sources of ire

Gretton – Rockingham – Great Easton – Bringhurst – Cottingham – Middleton – East Carlton – Wilbarston – Stoke Albany

As you come into Gretton check out the Pocket Park opposite Gretton House, a two-acre former paddock. The village is perched high on top of a vantage point overlooking the Welland Valley. When you reach the war memorial on your left, there is a welcome bench on which you can take a breather. Here pride (if that is the word) of place goes to the stocks and whipping post, a reminder of different times when summary justice was all the rage and petty larceny was swiftly dealt with by the local constable.

I'm not a violent woman, but must confess I stood a while and wrote a mental list of offenders I should like to see dealt with here: people who litter, those who tie bags of dog-poo to trees, anyone who parks on yellow lines with their hazard lights on, house-proud town-mice who favour plastic grass over the real thing, and anyone who buys ready-grated cheese. I also brought to mind some specific individuals who have crossed me, often without realising it, but I won't name and shame here.

When you're ready to set off again, wind your way through the village and look for the turn on your right to pick up the footpath again by Westhill Farm. At the end of the first field, stop and take in the magnificent view before you begin your descent. Go under the railway bridge then take a short left off the bridleway.

As the path veers right, Rockingham Castle comes into view up ahead. Built on the instruction of William the Conqueror, it has been continually occupied for around a thousand years. For the last 450 or so years, it has been the home of the Saunders-Watson family, who still live there, but it is also a wedding venue and tourist destination. Don't be fooled by the Leicestershire postcode, which cynics might say has been adopted to avoid the castle being associated with nearby former steel town Corby. It is definitely in Northamptonshire. You will, though, cross into Leicestershire on the way to Great Easton in a moment, and you can see four counties from the castle grounds: Northamptonshire, Lincolnshire, Leicestershire and Rutland.

The footpath comes out through the Estate Yard, just below the castle at the foot of Rockingham Hill. Turn right into the village, past the Sondes Arms. If you want to make a detour into the castle itself, turn left instead, but be warned that it is a very steep walk up the hill. The path picks up again between the pub and the village teashop. As you set off across the fields, look to your left and you will see the castle between the trees. I must admit, it looks quite splendid.

I have an uneasy relationship with the local landowners and while I love walking in the countryside I'm not sure I'm cut out to live there; but I'm a fan of *The Archers*, so I know a group of beaters when I come across them on a footpath, and this happened on one of our recent walks. We were following a route around one of the county's many Big Houses that took us into some lovely hidden villages, when we came upon a group of people who greeted us with a hearty 'Good morning' and reassurance that we would be quite safe on our walk because the guns would be pointing the other way. Always good to know.

Anyway, when you reach the road, jink across it and pick up the path (signposted Bridleway). The route now takes you through a tree plantation, then you will come up against the path of a disused railway, the route of the line that I'm fairly sure formerly ran from Peterborough to Market Harborough. I am indebted to friend and railway author Will Adams for the following confirmation:

'The line was part of a complex of lines in that area. There was a Midland Railway line from Peterborough via Stamford, and a London & North Western Railway line from Peterborough via Kingscliffe ('Over the Alps', as it was very hilly). An LNWR line left the MR line at Luffenham, and joined the other LNWR line at Seaton Junction; the line then ran through Rockingham to Market Harborough (and thence lines west to Rugby and south to Northampton). Well, you did ask…'

Thanks, Will.

Cross and keep going then turn left on to the unsurprisingly named Station Road. At the end of Gatehouse Lane, turn left at The Sun pub and walk into Great Easton.

The footpath skirts the southern edge of this pretty little village where many of the houses are built from local ironstone and topped either with Collyweston stone or long-straw thatch. Given the heads up by friends who had done the route before us, we sought out Furleigh Cottage, one of the oldest houses in the village and Grade II listed. It has a thatched canopy over the door and an owl built into its thatched roof.

The first time Mr Thorley and I walked this route was very nearly the last time. We had set off to do a linear walk from Gretton to Great Easton. This was in the days before we were fully fledged environmentalists and I'm now rather ashamed to say we drove in tandem to the end of the proposed walk and dropped off Mr Thorley's car. Then he got in with me and we drove to the start, the plan being that at the end of our walk he could give me a lift back to my car.

Having explored the delights of Gretton and taken some smashing photographs, we began our descent across the fields to Rockingham. Mother Nature had dusted off her Sunday best for us: we saw red kites and kestrels, and everywhere bows bent heavy with elderberries. In the shadow of Rockingham Castle, we enjoyed a delicious cream tea. Then, thus fortified, we strolled on to Great Easton, enjoying the diversity of colours and shades. It was all very idyllic.

However, just 200 yards from the end, it dawned on my dear husband that he had left his keys in my car six miles away. Yes, I know he didn't do it on purpose, but you'll understand why the walk back uphill took place in stony silence.

I wrote about the experience for the local paper, an exercise that secured me a regular column for a while. When the paper went from a daily to a weekly publication I was unceremoniously dropped. I'm not bitter.

The route out of Great Easton is clearly marked. Taking the stile on your left will lead you to a conservation area 'of land made available to the public for walking and quiet enjoyment'. A notice explains that the land is managed as a traditional Welland Valley Pasture and is used for the rearing of cattle and sheep. This field is crossed by a local footpath, should you wish to deviate. Look left for a last view of Rockingham Castle.

When you come out onto the road, turn right up the hill. A road sign marks the entrance to Bringhurst. Turn left towards the church of St Nicholas, which is perched right on top of the hill. Even the tiniest villages in Northamptonshire have substantial churches and the one in Bringhurst is a good example, with a splendid golden cockerel on its west tower. Truth be told, by the time we'd walked the whole footpath, Mr Thorley was getting fed up with seeing 'not another bloody cockerel' roosting aloft. Nevertheless, from its grounds there are stunning views across the Welland Valley.

Assuming you have a more tolerant walking companion, pause and look up. Then go round the church until you pick up the footpath again opposite the church gate. Near the top of the field is a clump of trees. Go to the left and follow the hedge until you reach a gap in the hedge, clearly marked for the Jurassic Way.

Now, I'm not saying Mr Thorley and I took an unexpected detour the first time we walked this stretch, but what I will say is that if you veer off to the right you will end up in Drayton, the little village you can see on the horizon. The footpath actually comes up through a private garden, but from there it is possible to follow a local footpath to the left and round in a circle to re-join the Jurassic Way further down the hill. If you go the 'correct' way you see this path joining on your right.

At the boundary of the last field before you cross a farm track and turn east towards Cottingham, you step back into Northamptonshire. A short distance on, steps up and down clearly show the path of the dismantled railway you will have crossed earlier on your way in to Great Easton.

At the junction with the public bridleway, turn left. The soft going underfoot gradually gives way to a rather unpleasant gravel path with some nasty potholes and signs of flytipping. The OS map names this as Occupation Road. At the wide bridge, if you look over the metal railings you will see Cottingham sprawled ahead of you on your left. That is your next destination.

You will need to dive into a gap in the hedge on your left for a brief but unpleasant walk past the water treatment works, which eventually leads you to the playing fields and then skirts the edge of a residential area. When you reach the road and turn right into the village, pass the Hunting Lodge. At the school, you can either go straight on for a more direct route to Middleton – it's hard to tell where one village ends and the other begins – but to stick to the Jurassic Way you need to go left into High Street.

Turn right at what was the Spread Eagle. Like many village inns, this one has been closed for some years. It seems such a shame, but while it is tempting to blame 'them' for its demise, the sad truth is that we are all partly responsible. The cliché 'use it or lose it' holds good here. If we continue to drink at home rather than going out, then of course places like this will close. Even before Covid-19, numbers of in-pub drinkers were dropping, and when supermarket beer is so cheap, can any of us be surprised? Of course, the fact that it's so easy to socialise (if that's the word) online means we no longer have to pop out for a swift half just to see who's about. Then there's the drink-driving aspect. As a much younger woman, I used to enjoy driving to a country pub and sitting in the beer garden with a glass of something lovely. Now older and wiser, I won't have so much as half a lager if I'm driving, and rightly so.

The last time we walked this way, a hearty rambling group was gathering outside the pub, eager to offer us advice on which way we should be going. We clearly looked lost even though we weren't, or perhaps it was my furrowed brow as I scribbled down some notes that misled them. They were able to tell us that the Royal George, just up the road would be reopening soon under new ownership; I hope this is the case.

Anyway, this road will lead you towards Water Lane, which you will pass on the left. The two villages of Cottingham and Middleton were once supplied with drinking water from nearby springs, with fountains and pumps at intervals along the way. Some of these still have a trickle of water flowing through them; I cannot vouch for its safety.

Climb the steep steps up to the church of St Mary Magdalene of Cottingham-cum-Middleton and prepare for yet more pretty views across the countryside and down to Middleton. If you're lucky enough to be able to get into the church (we've never managed it), you will be confronted with some amazing architecture, including curious capitals on its columns featuring women in wimples, knights and a bishop. Pride of place, though, goes to the Parish Chest, one of four so-called Watford Chests, made in the Northamptonshire village of that name that the Jurassic Way passes through later.

I'm not a church-goer, but I like to look around them in awe at the craftsmanship of the builders. I also like nosing around outside. Mr Thorley is not a big fan of graveyards, finding them somewhat unsettling. I can spend ages in them, marvelling at the old-fashioned names – when did you last come across a Bertha? – and making up stories based on the inscriptions on the headstones. I stood a while and pondered the sadness of one lady who survived her husband by 19 years. That's a long time to be on your own. A quick calculation revealed that she was 14 years younger than him, so it can't have been a complete surprise that he went so much sooner than she. Who knows. Perhaps she was sick of him.

At the east end of the graveyard is a Commonwealth War Grave for Colonel George Eustace Ripley, Northamptonshire Regiment 6th Bn, who died in October 1916, aged 52.

Middleton is tiny, virtually just the main street. In the 2011 census its population was recorded as 414. The steep hill pulling out to the south-west is known locally as The Hill. So many village houses have names that offer poignant reminders of their past: the Old School House, The Post House and so on. One example in Middleton is the Old Brewery. At this discovery, Mr Thorley sighed and expressed a vain wish to buy it and turn it into a new brewery in which he could pursue his ever-expanding interest in home-brewing. I appreciate there is little demand these days for, say, a blacksmith, but it does seem sad that so many of these crafts and trades have gone. I wonder if a hundred years' time, we shall see homes named The Coder's Retreat or Bitcoin Manor.

Opposite what was the Red Lion pub (now closed and at the time of our last visit an Indian restaurant, Nazz Spice) is a sign for a footpath to Wilbarston. This path goes down the edge of East Carlton Park, and while it doesn't go into the park or the village from which it gets its names, it is one of my favourite places in the north of the county, and there are several openings on the left that enable a detour into the park. At the very least it's a handy place to pause for a pee and a cuppa, but there is much more to it than that.

The nearby town of Corby is known for its steelworks and ironstone quarrying, and there is much evidence of that heritage in the park. When we first moved to the area, our two young sons were able to clamber on the retired engine and huge digger bucket at the top of the park; now they have been fenced off (the pieces of equipment, not my sons), so all you can do is stand and admire them. Seems a shame.

There is a great play area, some marked footpaths through the woods and down by the lake, punctuated by fabulous wooden carvings, and you can stand on the bridge and feed the ducks. There is open grass for ball games and plenty of space for picnics. A converted coach house and stables now house a great little café, together with workshops and exhibition space.

The café is occasionally closed, so if lack of a latte will spoil your day, check before you set off. Also note that while parking is free, when it's muddy quite a bit of the grass will be cordoned off, so you might have to park in the village.

There is plenty of outdoor seating and I enjoy sitting here people-watching while Mr Thorley goes off in search of a pot of tea and a toilet, not necessarily in that order. Sometimes while I'm waiting, I dig out my pen and notebook, because I have had what I think is a good idea and need to write it down immediately if it is not to disappear into the ether. I have a notebook on my bedside table, too, and often just as I'm dropping off I'll think of that perfect word or the idea for what I'm sure will lead to a place on the best-seller list. I scribble something down, and then in the morning wonder what on earth it meant and what made it so imperative to note down 'purple bedsocks' or 'no label on the coryopteris'.

Occasionally I use my phone for quick note-taking, but the challenge of tapping out sentences on those tiny keys is too much for fingers that can't keep up with my brain and I often end up with an incomprehensible string of gibberish. I also have a voice recorder, but hearing my random thoughts played back in my own voice is rarely a pleasant experience, especially if I can I was on the move and out of breath.

Anyway, I'm scribbling away trying to tether a thought when an ostentatious cough from the next table stymies the flow.

'Writing, are you?'

I try not to look, but can't help a surreptitious look over my specs at the woman who has spoken. She is of a certain age, with implausibly blonde hair. She is dressed not for walking, but rather for a fashion shoot for walking. Our eyes meet, so I feel obliged to speak.

'Yes,' I say, and drop my gaze to my paper.

'What is it: a poem? I like that Pam Ayres.'

And so in spite of my better judgement, I engage, albeit tersely.

'No, a book.'

She presses on.

'I've always fancied writing a book. Perhaps I will when I get time.'

I bristle. Occasionally, I'm invited to give talks to writing groups, the WI, the U3A and the like, and as part of my patter I have a list of 'Ten Things Never to Say to a Writer'. She has just uttered one of them. I mean, writing a book is only a matter of having a few minutes to spare every now and then, isn't it? It's not a matter of talent, or inclination or blood, sweat and tears.

I am this close to faking a phone call from my agent when Mr Thorley returns with a tray bearing not just a pot of tea but also the inevitable sausage roll for him and a slab of sturdy flapjack for me. I give my interrupter a weary smile and turn away.

One of my aforementioned sons is now a drummer and has used this park as the backdrop for a music video. East Carlton Hall, which stands deserted in the centre of the parkland, surrounded by Heras fencing, provided a suitably spooky background for the narrative about a park keeper who goes rogue; the building is said to be haunted by the Lavender Lady. The hall was built in 1870 for the Palmer family, then in the 1920s was leased to the Firth family of Sheffield. It was sold to steel manufacturer Stewarts and Lloyd in 1934, and after the war (during which time its air raid shelters were used to protect S&L's documents), it was used to host management trainees and company guests.

Before you pick up the path again, step outside the park gates and take a look at the almshouses on Church Lane, originally built in 1668, but remodelled in the Tudor style 200 years later. East Carlton is tiny, with fewer than 300 residents. It is one of the so-called Thankful Villages, which saw all the men who went to serve in the First World War return home safely. There is another such village in the county, at Woodend near Towcester.

Assuming you've either returned to the Jurassic Way or never left it, with East Carlton Park on your left, continue on to Wilbarston. This stage of the walk is slightly more challenging underfoot, with undulating terrain that verges on steep, which is unusual for Northamptonshire. With East Carlton church behind you, a patchwork of farm land stretches to the horizon, all with the accompanying drone of the A427.

The route takes you into Wilbarston by way of the football pitch past the recreation ground and the village hall and out on to the main road. Mr Thorley and I always pause here and reminisce about chilly Sunday mornings spent watching Number Two son playing Weetabix League football for Weekley Rovers. It was surely the draughtiest pitch on the whole fixture list.

Keep on the road and turn right into Church Street, passing the church. Before you know it, you'll come upon the village green in Stoke Albany.

Jurassic Way

5. Interlude
Shall we go for a walk?

If the coronavirus pandemic taught us nothing else, it confirmed that walking is good for the body, mind and soul. In Rebecca Solnit's fabulous book *Wanderlust* in which she quotes Leslie Stephen (Virginia Woolf's father): 'Walking is the best of panaceas for the morbid tendencies of authors.' And it's not just authors, of course. We all benefit from a breath of fresh air, especially now as we emerge from our enforced extended hibernation.

We tend to think of going for a walk as a country pursuit, but an urban walk can be equally rewarding, just different. It's often easier underfoot, for instance, and provides the opportunity to notice changes in one's local environment (including planning applications posted on lamp posts that might otherwise be approved unchallenged). It is not without its challenges, however. On one occasion walking down an alleyway beside a former shoe factory that has been converted into flats, there on the steps outside the main entrance were two people engaged in what can only be described as a sex act. I pretended not to notice.

There are many different words for walking: hiking, rambling, ambling, striding, sauntering, strolling, yomping and so on. However, I believe the verb 'to kale' is of my own invention. It means to go for a walk when not really in the mood, and is derived from the vegetable, which no one expects to enjoy despite knowing it will do them good.

Much of the time, if I'm not walking on my own, I only have Mr Thorley for company, which is how I like it. It's not that after 40+ years together we've run out of things to say, but rather that we don't feel the need to say anything at all. Many's the time we don't speak for miles at a stretch, and not just because we're out of breath or concentrating hard on putting one foot in front of the other without going flying. But after a while a thought will erupt from the mouth of one of us, and it's invariably a blurb from an internal monologue that seems completely random. For example, he might suddenly say, 'Of course, I'll have to give him a ring when I get back to see how it went.' Which is clearly the end of a long train of thought that has kept him quiet for the past 20 minutes.

Worryingly, or perhaps reassuringly, it doesn't usually take me long to cotton on to where he's been in his head.

'Yes,' I reply, 'and ask how Angie is, too.'

If I don't know what he's burbling on about, I acknowledge the outburst with a noncommittal 'Hmm,' and we walk on.

No matter how many people are in a group, each one is essentially doing his or her own private walk. We each have a different reason for walking – to get somewhere, to see something, for the exercise, for the mental benefits, to tick off a list like the Munros – so if you're thinking of joining a walking group you need to pick one carefully.

One of my friends told me a horror story about how she had been leaning on a tree after climbing up a particularly challenging hill, having a mindful pause with her eyes closed, when the moment was ruined by another member of the walking group coming up close and shouting 'Wake up!' in her ear.

There are two reasons why I don't like walking with a group and particularly with a group of strangers. The first is pace. I have short legs, but they're sturdy and I like to get a move on when I walk, not to the detriment of taking in my surroundings – I spotted a shrew the other day – and I like to stop and admire the view, particularly on a long slog uphill; but if we're walking, we're walking, people! I cannot abide a dawdler, and I think it's much more tiring to walk slowly than at a reasonable lick. Others will disagree and prefer to saunter in a way I would call aimless.

I used to belong to a group comprised of people who were lovely, but couldn't go for more than 30 minutes without stopping for a cake break. I once joined them for what was advertised as 'a good walk followed by a pub lunch'. On the day, I was disappointed when the walk turned out to be only two-and-a-half miles and the old-school pub didn't offer much in the way of a vegetarian option. On the menu, underneath Roast Beef, Spring Lamb and Chicken Casserole was quite simply 'Vegetarian dish'. Imagine the opposite: Falafel Burgers, Mushroom Risotto, Vegetable Lasagne and 'Meat'.

The other reason is the chat. Don't misunderstand me: I'm not saying that people shouldn't talk at all. Indeed, I've known people meet the love of their life on the towpath, but I'm not a fan of talking for talking's sake. I don't want to have to make small talk with people I don't know and might never see again.

It's not that I'm unsociable – OK, perhaps it is – but rather than when I'm out there I don't want to know what's going on in their heads. I have enough trouble with what's going on in mine.

I relish the connection with the natural world, the sense of being outside of normal life, just the whole feeling of otherness frees up the mind and allows it to wander or find stillness, whatever it needs. I can withdraw into my own internal world. It gives me space to think, to solve problems, to plan. The yoga teacher in me loves the concept of walking as a meditative process. It is a fantastic opportunity to observe the amazing connection between body and (shortness of) breath.

I have thought long and hard about the possibility of a silent walking group (patent pending). A group of people would gather in a car park, say, brief introductions would be made and heads counted, so that we don't lose anyone along the way, and the route and destination outlined. Watches might be synchronised for those for whom such things matter. Then we would stop talking and set off. Obviously if someone totters over the edge of a ravine or twists an ankle on a tussock, it would be OK to call out for assistance, but otherwise no talking allowed.

6. Horses, sheep, bulls and mountains
Stoke Albany – Braybrooke – Great Oxendon – East Farndon – Sibbertoft – Welford – Elkington – Winwick – West Haddon – Watford

Inside St Botolph's Church in Stoke Albany there is a memorial to the US Armed Forces. On 28th July 1941, XC Sqn Flying Fortress AN534 WP-E 28/07/41 departed Polebrook (about 40 miles away) for a high-altitude test flight. During the flight, the aircraft suffered catastrophic structural failure and broke up over Stoke Albany. All the crew were killed, including a serving member of the USAAF. As the USA had not entered the war at this point, he was not initially included in the casualty lists; he was added later, but only listed as an 'Observer'. Pay your respects, then resume your journey.

Don't be concerned that the signs seem to be directing you on to the A417. At the end of the slip road, a sign directs you to the welcome sight of a set of steps cut into the steep bank, which is your escape route back to the green fields. However, you will need to take extreme care, as the traffic will be approaching from behind you and probably building up speed in anticipation of the major road ahead. It is possible to clamber up the bank and walk there instead, but it is prickly in summer and slippery in winter.

In a short time, you will plunge briefly into the outskirts of Brampton/Stoke Wood, which is under the care of the Woodland Trust. The Stock Wood End Quarter is a nature reserve that is a wildlife haven, part of a larger woodland noted for the variety of its plant life, including twayblade, which I must confess I'd never heard of, but it turns out is a type of orchid.

At the edge of Brampton Wood, the path is joined by the Midshires Way, a long-distance footpath and bridleway that runs for 230 miles from the Chiltern Hills to Stockport, and the Macmillan Way, 290 miles long from the Lincolnshire fens to Dorset, which was devised to raise funds for Macmillan Cancer Support.

Now it's a matter of making steady progress up the long drag that leads to Hermitage Wood on the right and out on to the lane. Turn left and you will see Hermitage Cottages on your right, and just past here there is a soft grass cut-through that is a better option than following the marked path alongside the main road. In fact, the last time we did this stretch, some wag had turned around the official Jurassic Way signpost, directing the unwary towards Desborough. If you find yourself walking past a dreary motel on your left you've been had. Turn around now!

Assuming you've managed to navigate your way to the roundabout, take great care as you cross and then continue downhill across the fields. This is a bit of a weird stretch. For one thing, the footpath brings you into the yard of a swanky-looking stable, but rest assured you haven't gone wrong. Turn right and the metal gate will bring you on to the road. Be warned, however, there is such a jumble of roadworks and related nonsense here that seems to have been going on forever that it can be rather disconcerting. Courage, mon brave. Cross over and carry on downhill, pass under the railway line, then across the fields and out on the road.

Before you turn right for the short walk into Braybrooke, look behind you to where you have just walked and to the left you will see an elevated footbridge to take walkers on the Macmillan Way up and over the railway, affording grand views. A thought for another day, perhaps?

You will also be looking over the grounds of the medieval moated manor house known as Braybrooke Castle. You will easily spot the rise and fall of the land, which are the outlines of where buildings stood. However, if you look on Google Earth, you will be amazed at the detailed outline that still remain, albeit hidden beneath the surface. The castle was demolished in the early 1960s because it was in poor condition. What remains are the earthwork and buried remains of the castle and its associated enclosures and water control features.

Ignore the local footpath and walk down the road and into the village. You might be surprised to find yourself crossing the river Jordan here. Don't worry, you haven't fallen through a wormhole to the Middle East; this is a small tributary of the Welland. I have been told that the name comes from the fact that back in the 18th century the local Baptist Church would dam the river and use the collecting water in baptism ceremonies. I don't know if this is true, and would be happy to have the story confirmed or disproved. Either way, a plaque on the parapet records that the bridge dates from the 13th century, begun by Sir

Thomas Latimer of Braybrooke Castle, which is impressive in itself.

The village isn't very big, but is proud of its history. The Braybrooke Tapestry is a beautiful piece of needlework art depicting key historical events in Braybrooke from 1000 to 2000 AD. Each panel was created by someone in the community, and the finished work was displayed in the village hall.

The Jurassic Way collides again with the Macmillan Way and Midshires Way here. If you lose your bearings, head for the church, then follow Newland Street downwards. The lane is marked as a dead end, but at the end you will pick up the Jurassic Way. This can be a very slippery uphill stretch, because there is a lot of farm and smallholding activity in the vicinity.

The next settlement will be Great Oxendon, and the route there is a lovely mixture of field and woodland, footpaths and roadways. This is very horsey countryside, including one part that goes through a property with lots of horses in the field through which the footpath goes. On our visit, one horse was standing guard right in the middle of the path, but we managed to pass by unscathed.

The thing about horses is they are often kept within electric fencing, a fact that we found out the hard way on one occasion. Pausing to check the map, I was disturbed by Mr Thorley shouting 'Bastard!' and leaping up in the air clutching his arm. He shouldn't have touched the fence, of course, but in his defence the point at which we had to cross it was by a rickety stile and it was a bit hairy. I laughed at the time (once I'd checked he was OK, of course), but a while later I did a similar thing. Trying to swing myself around a gate post to avoid a particularly well-poached patch of mud, I started to topple and reached out to an electrified fence to steady myself. It was Mr Thorley's turn to laugh.

We've had a few Chuckle Brothers moments with sheep, too. One day, we walked through a really wide field where there was a small flock of sheep at either end. As we set off, both groups walked towards the middle, paused for a moment, then carried on walking, so those that were formerly at the top were now at the bottom. Then they all turned round and looked towards the middle of the field. It looked for all the world as though they were changing ends at half-time in some woolly team game. Having had a laugh at their expense, we walked on towards the gate on the other side, at which point both teams turned to follow us towards the gate, clearly expecting something that we were not equipped to provide. We laughed nervously, not frightened, but certainly glad to reach the boundary and put a sturdy barrier between them and us.

Less amusing was the time we followed the signs correctly only to be confronted with a notice warning us 'Beware of the bull'. Sure enough, the creature was very much in evidence in the field, so we turned round. This makes me cross, because I'm very respectful of the countryside and those for whom it is their workplace. I leave gates as I find them and don't interfere. Almost without exception, landowners leave a clear way across their fields for walkers to follow either by mowing or guiding with planting or fencing. Occasionally, though, there will be a little detour – for instance, you might be directed around the edge of a field, rather than straight across it. I tend not to be belligerent about ramblers' rights, and will respect the farmer's wishes and follow the alternative route. It is therefore annoying when there is a tonne of prime beef in my legitimate way. I know there are people who say cows are more dangerous than bulls, but I'm not prepared to take my chances with either. That's one of the reasons I recommend carrying the OS map with you, in case you have to find your way past a snorting obstacle.

On the outskirts of Great Oxendon you cross the Brampton Valley Way, a 14-mile recreational route for walkers, cyclists and horse riders on what was formerly a branch line run by the London and North Western Railway. It is part of Sustrans National cycle route 6. It incorporates the Oxendon Tunnels, which are accessible, but you will need a torch. You'd be surprised how difficult it is to walk or cycle in the dark!

The Jurassic Way runs parallel to the village's main street, then goes north and north-west towards East Farndon along a single-track road, so take care. This is easy walking, so why not take a couple of short detours? About a mile out on the right is a track to the site of Little Oxendon, although in all honesty there's not a lot to see beyond ridge and furrow remnants. There is a much better example of a lost medieval village just beyond Sibbertoft (see next chapter).

The other detour a little further on and on the other side of the route is to Rupert's Viewpoint. It was to this ridge that on the morning of 14th June 1645 King Charles I and Prince Rupert brought the royal army up from Market Harborough. What followed that day was the Battle of Naseby, the decisive battle of the Civil War during which parliament's New Model Army destroyed King Charles's main field army. Only about 4,000 Royalists escaped the field, most of whom were either cavalry or senior officers; the main Royalist field army was destroyed.

South of here, the A14, which connects the M1 and the A1, goes straight through the site of the battle, which seems remarkably disrespectful given its significance. The village of Naseby is south of the main road, from which a B-road takes you to Fairfax's Viewpoint for the opposite perspective. For now, though, stick to the path and you'll come into the southern end of East Farndon.

East Farndon is another linear village, built along a single road that goes north to Market Harborough. There is a(nother!) golden cockerel on the top of East Farndon Church, but this fact was lost on the drivers of the procession of cars that we watched screech to a halt in the pull-in in front of the church while we were taking a breather. Teams of three and four were in hot pursuit on a car treasure hunt – is this still a good idea, given that we are trying to save the planet, I wondered – looking for a memorial to tick off on their crib sheet. We watched from the safety of the little green space in front of the church, where we could quite clearly see what they were looking for;

there is a wooden bench inscribed to the memory of George Marriott 'who helped fund and care for this land'.

The route takes a bit of a loop here that on paper looks like it might not be worth the effort. However, I urge you to do it, because it takes you up on to a hilltop where there is a cracking view of the surrounding farmland. We joined a local man who was there just to have a look. He told us that he and his beautiful black Labrador often walk up here to check on nature's progress through the seasons. On the day we were there, an enormous combine harvester was trekking to and fro, kicking up an awful lot of dust across what our new friend told us the locals call the Rabbit Field.

We commented on the huge number of horses we had seen in his neck of the woods. Turns out that many of them are owned not by local people, but by out-of-towners who buy the land for their animals.

One of the notable things about this walk is that we met very few people doing it, except in the villages themselves. It was nice to stand and chat with this gent, and from this vantage point he was able to indicate where the next stile was and which way we should walk. We went back towards East Farndon, then followed the route as it skirted round the hill in a gentle sweep, then crossed another B-road at the junction with a path coming in from the north, before creeping on to Sibbertoft.

Follow the footpath on the OS map and as you come into the patch of woodland called The Lawn, you will notice that over to the south-east there is an area called Castle Yard on which is marked the site of remains of a motte and bailey probably dating from the Norman Conquest. However, the only way to get to this spot is along a private farmyard – and the 'keep out' message is quite firm!

The footpath comes out on the road, takes a turn left then leads into St Helen's churchyard. A few yards in, on the left, is the grave of the Reverend Miles Joseph Berkeley, a 19th-century botanist responsible for Outlines of British Fungi and Introduction to Cryptogramic Botany. He must have been a wow at parties. I shouldn't mock; he was an important fellow in his field, and even had a genus of algae named after him, Berkeleyea. If you have a yen to pay further homage to him, there is a plaque in his honour on the wall of the Old Rectory. Find this by going back out of the churchyard the way you came and continue on down past the playground and war memorial, turn right into Berkeley Street and the old rectory is almost at the end of the road, on the left.

The village hall in Sibbertoft glories in the name of The Reading Room, which pleases me no end. Further points of interest are that there is a spring in the village that is the source of the Welland, and Sibbertoft was on Charles Stuart's final approach to the Battle of Naseby.

Back to the churchyard. Follow the path round and you will see a stile in the far corner. Over the hill from Sibbertoft, the path takes you on a quiet trek towards the hamlet of Sulby and then on to the site of the medieval village of Old Sulby. Even on the ground, the humps and hollows are clear to see (much better than Little Oxendon), but take a look at it on Google Earth and the detail is astonishing. Alternatively, get in touch with the gliding centre in Sibbertoft and, who knows, you might be able to negotiate a trip out that way.

For this stage of the journey, the path coincides with the waymarked Reservoir Walk, and sure enough up ahead through the trees we caught the glint of the sun reflecting off the water. A concrete bridge takes the route between Sulby and Welford reservoirs, overseen by the Canals & Rivers Trust. Sulby Reservoir is the higher of the two and provides water to the summit level of the Grand Union Canal by way of the navigable Welford Arm.

Our next stop, Welford, is the largest village we have been to for quite some time. It is bisected by the A5199, the main road between Northampton and Leicester, and as such was in the past a major staging post halfway along the route. It is also the first settlement on the Avon. The Jurassic Way actually goes around to the west of Welford, just tucking into its bottom edge, veering off to the left along Naseby Road. However, if you follow the road to the right instead, you can walk through the village in search of a brew, then pick up the footpath at the other end of High Street.

There are no huge hills to climb along the Jurassic Way, but the next section includes the wooded ridge of Hemplow Hills, which might surprise you.

What might surprise you even more is that there are 72 hills in the county that are considered by some to be mountains. There is no official definition of when a hill becomes a mountain; rather, it is more a case of how far above the surrounding land it sticks up. BBC Bitesize, rather vaguely says mountains are 'higher and usually steeper than a hill and are generally over 600m high'. That seems rather low to me, given that Snowden (Yr Wyddfa) has an elevation of 1,085 metres/3,560 feet and a prominence of 1,038 metres/3,406 feet. Still, you take what you can get.

Stride on along the stretch known as Hemplow Drive towards Hemploe (sic) Lodge Farm and West Hill Farm then upwards. Before you dip down again on the other side, take in the view. If you can look beyond the mighty A14 you will see Honey Hill in the distance. This is one of the county's so-called mountains at 214 metres/702 feet above sea level with a prominence of 68 metres/223 feet. Again, not huge, but one of the highest points on the whole of the Jurassic Way. There is more about Honey Hill anon.

Then descend towards the Grand Union Canal, for what is one of my favourite stretches of the walk. The Jurassic Way joins the towpath and goes under the A14, and I love the juxtaposition of a canal boat taking the slow route while just above it a 44-tonne truck is hurtling towards Felixstowe.

Once under the road you walk around Cot Hill to Heygate's Lodge. The canal continues southwards, but the footpath goes into the tiny hamlet of Elkington, which is pretty much just one farm. However, it proved a useful parking spot for a recent adventure, inspired by an article in Country Walking magazine, which reported that Cold Ashby in

Northamptonshire was the site of the first trig point, built in 1936. The mention of this village reminded me of a trip there in the early 1980s, when we had only recently moved to the county. It had snowed, a lot, so the enterprising golf club in the village had opened up its course to skiers. A small but effective drag lift had been installed and we spent a couple of hours chugging up and hurtling down what the golfers call Cardiac Hill.

What better excuse, then, for a walk to find said trig point. It is clearly marked on the OS map, we planned to follow the Jurassic Way up Honey Hill, then go along the lane and take a picture. We set off in good order, but were defeated by mud up to our knees on a narrow track that had been made all the worse by the churning of a motorbike scrambler, so we thought we'd attack it from the other end. However, we were thwarted again on finding that the trig point was just out of sight behind the industrial architecture of a reservoir station. Not having the nerve to brave the (unlocked) security gate, we contented ourselves with a mean and moody photo of the area. Nevertheless, it wasn't a completely wasted trip, because we walked instead from Elkington in the other direction along the towpath to the multimodal spot I described above.

Follow the path out of Elkington up Honey Hill and then down again. At the top of the hill is a stone bearing a plaque that commemorates the opening of the Jurassic Way on 19th September 1994. It seems rather an odd place to have done this, but I suppose it is pretty much halfway along the route, and it is a lovely spot. I wonder how the councillors named on the plaque enjoyed the climb.

Cold Ashby Golf Club will be on your left. Cold Ashby itself is a mile or so to the east, so if you want to visit what claims to be the highest village in Northamptonshire, lying as it does on the 200 metres/656 feet contour line, you will have to leave the Jurassic Way and walk down the lane.

Between here and the next village, Winwick, there is little of note in the way of structures, so it's an ideal stretch to breathe in deep and lose yourself in your thoughts.

Winwick is tiny – Wikipedia calls it a 'lost settlement', which seems a little harsh – though it is true that a single postcode covers the whole village. It does, though, have the remains of a 16th-century brick manor house and St Michael's & All Angels' Church.

During the coronavirus pandemic, from March 2020 a community magazine was set up to keep residents informed and entertained. The Winwick Warbler was awarded a Rose of Northamptonshire Award, presented as part of the Unsung Heroes initiative launched by the Lord Lieutenant and the High Sheriff and recognising contributions made by people who lived and worked in Northamptonshire during the pandemic.

Keep going until you climb the hill into West Haddon, one of the larger villages on our route. The bulk of the village is on the east side of the path, which goes into the centre, takes a little loop and then continues westwards. The Pocket Park is on Old

Forge Drive, next to the playing field on the south-eastern edge of the village. The fields of West Haddon were the location for an enclosure riot in 1765. An advertisement was made in the county newspaper for a football game that was to be played in those fields, but in fact this was just a way to assemble a mob to protest against the fencing in of common land.

Evidence of later turbulent times is to be seen in a milestone to which a notice was added in 2004, commemorating the fact that the details had been deliberately obscured during the Second World War so any passing enemy wouldn't know it was 11 miles to Northampton and 77 miles to London.

If you are lucky enough to be able to get into All Saints Church, in the south aisle by the doorway you will be able to see the extraordinary Norman font that was discovered in 1887, built into the west wall of the nave. It is damaged in some places – hardly surprising given its 12th-century origins – but has been placed on a modern stand, and the faces, each carved with a figure in relief with a beaded upper border, are there to be admired.

The route out of West Haddon takes us on another stretch of quiet countryside, passing Silsworth Lodge, Flavell's Lodge and skirting the Watford Covert (a covert is a thicket in which game can hide). To the east of the path you will be able to see the mighty turbines of the Watford Lodge Windfarm.

Now you are about to reach one of the route's most surprising destinations, Watford.

7. Mulitmodal transport and a Guy Fawkes apologia

Watford –Ashby St Ledgers – Braunston – Staverton – Lower Catesby – Hellidon – Charwelton – Church Charwelton – Woodford Halse

I f the words 'Watford Gap' mean service station to you, you will find the village of Watford a pleasant surprise. Like so many of the places on our route, on paper it looks as though there will be nothing of note, but despite it being laid on pretty much a single S-shaped road, the village boasts several listed buildings. Among them is the Church of St Peter and St Paul, believed to have been founded in around 1300. It underwent extensive restoration in 2013/14, and the graveyard has also been cleaned, revealing headstones that had been hidden for decades. Just north of the village (which you will pass on the way in) is Watford Park, the remains of an 18th-century garden overlying the shrunken medieval village of Watford and associated ridge and furrow cultivation.

The real highlight, though, is the Watford Locks, another of my favourite spots on the route. Follow the path out of the village and past Bluebell Spinney, under the motorway, and suddenly there you are, in a time capsule of gentle living, with the chug-chug of boats on the Grand Union Canal, and the reassuring mechanical clunk of the winding gear as the paddles in the gates are shifted by the manual lock key called a windlass.

Thousands of people pass by this tranquil spot every day without even noticing it. The site is hemmed in by the M1, the A5 on the route of Watling Street, and the West Coast Main Line railway, which all speed through the gap in the hills that gives the nearby service station its name. Despite this, the site is peaceful. Settle on a bench and watch the world go by or walk along the towpath and watch as the canal traffic – if you can call it that – negotiates the lock system. Close your eyes and imagine you're back in 1814, when the locks first opened.

There is actually a series of seven locks on this section of the canal. From the southern end, there are two single locks, then four in a staircase, where the middle lock gate connects the top and bottom locks together, and then another single one. Only one boat can go through at a time and you will need the permission and guidance of the lock-keeper to make the trip from bottom to top. The total height of the system is 52 feet 6 inches, lifting boats up to the Leicester Summit for their journey onwards towards Foxton Locks and Leicester itself. On a clear run, the journey through the whole system will take about 45 minutes. Access is only possible at certain times (roughly Easter to October) to ensure that the locks aren't abused and to help keep down queues.

There's no gift shop, although there are some leaflets in the lock-keeper's station, and no refreshment room, unless you count the water tap. There's nothing to do except sit.

Eventually you will have to stir yourself and get back to the business of walking. The footpath turns off the towpath, you clamber over a stile to pass under the A5 and the railway and set off towards Ashby St Ledgers.

The church in Ashby St Ledgers is dedicated to the Blessed Virgin Mary and St Leodegarius, whom neither Mr Thorley nor I had heard of. We have since learned that he was a French Benedictine bishop and martyr of the 7th century. It is from him that the village gets its name; in France he is known as St Leger.

This is an extremely pretty village. In fact, a Conservation Area covers the whole of the village. If the church is open, it is easy to spend an hour or more exploring inside. We were lucky enough to be able to do this and were intrigued by the faint image of a skeleton painted in the west end of the nave on the arch.

But what attracts most visitors to the village is the Manor House. This building passed through several families from the time of William the Conqueror until eventually it was taken over by the Catesby family in the 14th century. William Catesby was Chancellor of the Exchequer to Richard III. Five generations later, Robert Catesby lived there with his mother and it is widely believed that it was in his home that the details of the Gunpowder Plot were conceived.

The Manor House later passed into the hands of the crown. In 1903, it was bought by Viscount Wimborne (more properly, Ivor Churchill Guest, 1st Viscount Wimborne, 1873–1939), who employed Sir

Edwin Lutyens to undertake improvements to the house and elsewhere in the village. He is buried in the churchyard, where his headstone acknowledges that he was: Baron Wimborne of Cranford Magna, Baron Ashby St Ledgers of Ashby St Ledgers, a baronet, an MP, Paymaster General, a lord in waiting to the king (George V) and Lord Lieutenant of Ireland (he was one of the last people to hold this post). William Catesby is also buried here.

The house is in private hands now, so try not to gawp, but take time to notice the beggars' seats built into the gatehouse.

Guy Fawkes: an apologia

The transition of King James VI of Scotland to James I of England was not a happy one. He was unpopular with many English Catholics who felt that his laws were designed to control their rights. He needed some publicity that would show him in a better light or at least win him some sympathy. Step forward Guy Fawkes and his fellow Gunpowder Plot conspirators.

Fawkes was born in York in 1570. He was raised as a Protestant, but when he was 10 years old his stepfather persuaded him to convert and he became a zealous Catholic. In 1593, he joined the Catholic Spanish army to fight against the Protestant Dutch Republic and served until 1604. Then, at the invitation of Catholic gent Robert Catesby, he was smuggled back to England to unite in a conspiracy with Ambrose Rookwood, Everard Digby and

Francis Tresham. Fawkes joined the plotters because he considered the king to be a heretic. As he put it: 'Desperate diseases require desperate remedies.'

The plan was to destroy the king and his parliament by setting explosives under the Palace of Westminster during the opening of parliament on 5th November 1606. Fawkes was very skilful with explosives, so his role was to acquire and set the gunpowder and then detonate the blast.

Yet as it turned out, the king was never in any danger. Tresham and others, uneasy at the prospect of their friends being killed, betrayed their fellow plotters. It seems that the authorities decided to let the plan go ahead to catch them in the act of treason. Twelve hours before the king was due in parliament, soldiers, forewarned, searched the cellars and came across 36 barrels of gunpowder, with Fawkes in the act of laying the explosive. They arrested him.

Fawkes was unaware that he had been betrayed. Despite horrific torture on the rack, it was two days before he revealed his name and several more days before he gave up details of the plot and the names of the others involved, not knowing that they had already been identified and arrested or killed.

Fawkes was sentenced to the traditional traitor's death, namely to be hanged, drawn and quartered. However, when he stood on the gallows he jumped, thus breaking his neck and saving him from the agonies of being cut down and eviscerated while still alive. Even so, his body was cut up and sent to the four corners of the kingdom to warn others.

Far from removing a troublesome Protestant king, Fawkes was unwittingly part of a scheme that saw James I's position strengthened, while fear and hatred of the Catholics increased. Some sources even say the king respected Fawkes as a man of 'Roman resolution'.

Fawkes was neither the instigator nor the leader of the Gunpowder Plot, but his story caught the public imagination and his name remains synonymous with the event. It hardly seems fair. Catesby, the actual leader, was killed while trying to evade capture.

Right, after that history lesson it's time to clear your head by walking up and across the fields towards the next village, Braunston.

Braunston is where the Grand Union Canal and the Oxford Canal meet and is one of the busiest points on the British canal network. Nevertheless, there is an air of tranquillity here that cries out to be savoured. Luckily, the Admiral Nelson and Lock 3 is there to offer refreshments. Take some time to explore the spot, and look out for the Stop House, the old building where tolls used to be collected from passing freight boats.

On one visit to this stretch, as we sat outside the pub enjoying a lazy drink, a stream of runners jogged under the bridge and away along the towpath towards Daventry. Better-informed customers at the next table were able to tell us that they were taking part in the Grand Union Canal Race, 'Britain's longest, toughest, non-stop running race'. It is run along the waymarked towpath from Gas Street Basin in the centre of Birmingham to Little Venice in London along the Grand Union Canal, and competitors are required to complete the 145 miles within the time limit of 45 hours. The consensus among those of us watching was, 'Rather them than me!'

Incidentally, while the footpath into the town is well marked, if you decide to drive there to start a walk, parking on the route is a bit tricky. There is a car park at Top Lock, but only for patrons of the pub. Walking towards Home Farm, you will join the tow path for an easy stroll to the bridge, then turn right across the fields again.

The next chunk of the walk is in open, undulating countryside. You will skirt round the eastern edge of Braunston Covert before going virtually due south for just under 2 miles. Look east and you might catch a glimpse of the logistics centre in Daventry. Then come along the bridleway into Staverton and head for the village green. Last time we were there, there was a post marking the three-quarter point on the route: 66 miles from Stamford and 22 miles to Banbury.

This is a tiny village, but it has some beautiful buildings, many of which have amazing fossils in their walls. Oakham Lane is particularly splendid in this regard, and this is the point at which I usually threaten to leave Mr Thorley behind and continue on my own, because he can't tear himself away from the belemnites.

If you can lift your eyes from the fossils, there are views west across the river Leam into Warwickshire. On a clear day, you can see the Malvern and the

Shropshire Hills. Off the route to the east, along the Badby Road is Big Hill. This is Northamptonshire's biggest peak in terms of its height above sea level (235 metres/771 feet) and its prominence (114 metres/374 feet).

Staverton has one of the county's Pocket Parks, in Jetty Field off The Green, should you have time for a detour. The main field is managed to encourage a rich variety of grasses and wildflowers.

As you leave the village, the next point of interest is the Catesby Viaduct, which goes across the Leam at the end of the 300-yard tunnel that carried the Great Central Railway from Charwelton to Upper Catesby.

The path itself goes on to Lower Catesby. Although there are now only a handful of houses remaining, the village was the site of a priory until 1536, when Henry VIII had other ideas. Although the building went on to form part of the manor house, the present Catesby House (in private hands), halfway up the hill to the east of the village, was built in 1863.

Leaving Lower Catesby, the path goes over the Leam and runs parallel to it into Hellidon, which lies on the north face of an ironstone ridge. I'm smiling as I write this, but this is the area that has the greatest concentration of Northamptonshire's 'mountains'. The Jurassic Way doesn't cross them, but check your OS map and you will see over to the east between here and Charwelton are Studborough Hill, Arbury Hill, Little Down Hill and Sharman's Hill. Steppington Hill to the west isn't much to write home about, but it is on the list.

The highest point of Hellidon is Windmill Hill, at 208 metres/670 feet. Said windmill was built in 1842, but has long since stopped working. It was converted to a home for a while and then became the heart of a vineyard, but has now ceased trading.

Next stop is Charwelton, which takes us through an area of small hills. Off to the south, but not visible, is the site of a former quarry operated by the Park Gate Iron and Steel Company until 1961. From there, a mile-and-a-half mineral railway ran down the valley to bring ironstone to the main line at Charwelton station.

The path skirts the small village on its north-eastern, but the real point of interest is the packhorse bridge. Only 3 feet wide, it has two pointed arches, with low parapets so as not to impede the horses' panniers. In fact, this is what was formerly called Upper or Over Charwelton. This explains why the church is about a mile further on, in Church Charwelton, near the site of the medieval village of Charwelton. There are earthwork remnants of the former village around the church, and the remains of a set of fish ponds that were fed by the river.

Keep going across the dismantled railway and a little further on the right is Hinton Hill, another of the county's 'mountains', with a prominence of a mighty 39 metres/128 feet.

You will cross a stream by a footbridge on the outskirts of Woodford Halse. Then it's up the hill through the residential area, and down towards the former railway bridge.

Jurassic Way

8. Furballs and the home straight
Woodford Halse – Chipping Warden –
Edgecote – Wardington – Chacombe –
Middleton Cheney – Overthorpe –
Warkworth – Banbury

Until the railway came to Woodford Halse on 1899, it had been a tiny farming community, but it subsequently doubled in size and became a proper railway town. The line closed in 1966, but there is evidence of its presence in some of the buildings and in the bridge over Station Road. As you follow the path under the bridge on Station Road, a bricked-up entrance arch marks the position of the stairway that led to the island platform above.

The Pocket Park to the south-west of the town is a 17-acre reserve established in the railway cuttings that were once part of the Great Central Railway. It can be reached on foot down a permitted way on the left of the footpath about half a mile out of the town or by car on the Woodford Halse to Eydon road.

Having left behind the town, it's plain sailing across the countryside towards the site of the former medieval village of West Farndon. There are some earthwork remains, but little else. One time when walking this stretch I suddenly realised Mr Thorley wasn't behind me. I looked back and saw him holding on to a tree, coughing and spluttering like a cat trying to dislodge a particularly tenacious furball. Between splutters, he managed to explain that he'd swallowed a fly. I left him to it. Eventually, his breathing returned to normal and he caught up with me.

'You might have been a bit more sympathetic,' he grumbled.

Keep going and in a scant mile and a half the Jurassic Way meets several other footpaths. Make sure you follow the way to the west, uphill and then down Jobs Hill on to the road, before turning right into the beautiful village of Chipping Warden (the only 'Chipping' in the county, derived from an Old English word meaning market), which is now a conservation area. It was a medieval trading centre of some significance, as evidenced by the remains of the market cross beside the 14th-century church of St Peter and St Paul. The village marks the Northamptonshire end of the Battlefields Trail, a 20-mile marked footpath through the heart of England, from Chipping Warden to Kineton, Warwickshire. It links the sites of three battles: Edgecote (1469) in Northamptonshire, Cropredy Bridge (1644) in Oxfordshire and Edgehill (1642) in Warwickshire. There is an information board about this other footpath.

Just as you set off south across the fields, turn around to look back towards Chipping Warden and to the right of the path is another sad wartime monument, this time to the Second World War. On 18th April 1945, a Wellington bomber crashed here, killing five of its young crew, aged between 19 and 24. Only one, a 19-year-old, survived. A plaque honours their names.

As you arrive in the tiny village of Edgecote, the first thing you see is the splendid entrance to Edgecote House, built in the middle of the 18th century on the site of a much older house Edgecote Lodge, where it is thought Charles I spent the night before the Battle of Edgehill in 1642 during the English Civil War. The village to the west of the house was demolished by the Lord of the Manor in around 1780 to create a landscaped park. The church in Edgecote has a wonderfully wonky door.

Across the fields and up the hill and you will arrive in the north side of Wardington (known as Lower Wardington), which is actually just over the border into Oxfordshire. The path makes a loop past the manor house on its way to Upper Wardington, before breaking back into the countryside to continue on southwards, down the hill and across the stream that marks the county boundary back into Northamptonshire.

The walk into Chacombe village takes you over a wildflower meadow in an area known as the Berry Close Mound, a space maintained not only for the community, but also – if not primarily – for the wildflowers and the insects and wildlife they support. The lumps and bumps in the plot of land are clear indications of a fascinating past, and archaeological digs have revealed burnt wattle and daub and finds from the early Medieval, Saxon and Norman periods.

While we were walking this stretch, we fell into conversation with a local man who told us the meadow had previously been used for the grazing of rare sheep breeds. When the owner of the land died, she left it to the council. The sheep-owner had to quit and the field became the wildflower meadow you can see today.

In the village itself is a country house built on what was the site of an Augustinian priory, founded by Hugh de Chacombe during the reign of Henry II. There is some evidence of the priory site to the west.

Climbing out of the village, the path goes due south before taking a sharp turn eastwards toward Middleton Cheney, the largest town for quite a while. The first time we walked this stretch we arrived by car and were nearly defeated before we even started, because we couldn't find any seashell markers. However, the path is marked; we were just being dim. There is more testament to the county's violent past here, since this was the site of one of the first battles of the English Civil War, fought in May 1643, and it is possible that some of the fallen soldiers are buried in the town churchyard. All Saints Church has some fine stained glass, including some examples by Sir Edward Burne-Jones.

The route leaves the village by crossing over the A422 bypass, then making a sharp turn west towards Overthorpe. We are still in Northamptonshire, but only just: the western edge of the hamlet forms the boundary with Oxfordshire. There is no church in Overthorpe. It is in the Church of England parish of St Mary, Warkworth, whose 14th-century church is mid-way between the two villages, and the footpath goes past it. Inside, there the altar tomb of lord of the manor Sir John Lyons. I nearly lost Mr Thorley as we left Overthorpe, he kept stopping to admire the most extraordinary examples of fossils that were littering our way, almost as though they had been dropped there for him to find.

And now we're on the home straight, walking south-west over the railway line, under the M40 where we cross into Oxfordshire. Then we pick up the Oxford Canal path to turn north-west towards the finishing line in Banbury. It has to be said that the last couple of miles are not the prettiest, because they go through an industrial estate. At least on the level and it's impossible to get lost.

While the northern end in Stamford is marked with a proper stone monument, the southern end just sort of peters out. Arrive at Banbury Lock and you'll see the usual seashell sign, but there's nothing else. Don't despair though. Walk up into the town and take a look at the famous Banbury Cross. You won't be able to get very close, because it lies at the intersection of four major roads to Oxford, Warwick, Shipston-on-Stour and High Street. The current neo-gothic cross was put up in 1859 to commemorate the marriage of Queen Victoria's eldest daughter Victoria Adelaide Mary Louisa to Friedrich Wilhelm of Prussia on 25th January 1858. It is 52 feet 6 inches high to the top of its gilt cross and has niches for three statues.

Across the road and to the right is the Fine Lady herself perched on an anatomically correct stallion.

Ride a cock horse to Banbury Cross,
To see a fine lady ride on a white horse.
With rings on her fingers and bells on her toes,
She shall have music wherever she goes.

Resources

The following resources provided me with additional information and might do the same for you.

Who's Buried Where in Northamptonshire by Richard Cowley, Hooded Lion Books, 2000
Northamptonshire in a Nutshell by Ron Mears, Orman Publishing, 1995
English Parish Churches by Edwin Smith, Olive Cook and Graham Hutton, Thames & Hudson, 1976
50 Gems of Northamptonshire: The History & Heritage of the Most Iconic Places by Will Adams, Amberley Publishing, 2017

Useful websites

United Kingdom Amateur Fossil Hunters: www.ukafh.com
British Geological Survey: www.bgs.ac.uk
Easton-on-the-Hill: www.roll-of-honour.com/Northamptonshire/EastonOnTheHill.html
Pocket Parks: www.northamptonshireparks.co.uk/northamptonshire-pocket-parks
The Priest's House: www.nationaltrust.org.uk/priests-house-easton-on-the-hill
Ketton Cement Works: www.hanson-communities.co.uk/en/sites/ketton-community-page

Collyweston slate:
www.collywestonstoneslaterstrust.org.uk and
www.claudesmith.co.uk
Wakerley: www.visitchurches.org.uk
Harringworth: www.harringworth.org/history/the-railway-viaduct/
East Carlton: www.corby.gov.uk/leisure-culture/home/leisure-culture/parks-open-spaces/east-carlton-countryside-park
Stoke Albany: www.warmemorialsonline.org.uk
Great Oxendon: www.battlefieldstrust.com
Edgecote: www.battlefieldstrust.com

Many of the places along the route also have their own websites.

About the author

Julia Thorley is originally from Staffordshire, but is now based in Northamptonshire, a county she is happy to call home. As well as being a writer and editor, she can also sing a little, dance a little, play the piano and the ukulele, and sit in the Lotus position, though not necessarily all at the same time. Readers' thoughts and comments are welcome: criticisms, too, as long as they are gentle.

Website: www.juliathorley.com
Facebook: @JuliaThorleyAuthor
Twitter: @JThorleyAuthor

Other recent books by Julia Thorley

A Sparge Bag on the Washing Line
Tasting Strangers: A Collection
Stripped-back Yoga
Nine Lives: Monologues and first-person stories for reading aloud

Jurassic Way

Printed in Great Britain
by Amazon